Seducing the
Asparagus Queen

Cloudbank Books
Corvallis, Oregon

Seducing the Asparagus Queen

For
Emilyn~
Hope you
recognize
Milligan in
these
poems.

A 12/2018

By Amorak Huey

Cover photograph by Justin Hamm
Author photograph by Zoe-Kate Huey

1 2 3 4 5 6 7 8 9 0

Cloudbank Books
216 SW Madison Ave.
Corvallis, OR 97333
www.cloudbankbooks.com

For Ruth & Glen Adams
and for Howard & Reva Huey

Contents

Grail Bird

It is said the present is allotted seven seconds
before it becomes the past.
Now—now—then.
                              It's what we have.
I can live with this knowledge; I continue
to believe I have a choice. Imagine: the maybe-last

ivory-billed woodpecker in the world
lives in a white pine forest in eastern Arkansas;
one passionate searcher captured on film
its transcendental winged blur: a lifetime
of devotion rewarded by seven grainy seconds.

A reporter from Little Rock wondered:
Was it worth it?
                    Ask a tree if the sky proved
worth the rain—the roots—the ground. Ask lightning:
Was thunder worth the pain? Is that future worth
                              this past—

this undiscovered
                    glade of live oak and river birch
where sunlight angles green through summer leaves
and a dozen or a hundred or a million woodpeckers
sound their toy-trumpet call and staccato double rap—

                              now, and now, and now.

LIFE STORIES
AND OTHER POSSIBILITIES

Life Story

Born into a musical family.
Grew up under a rose tree.
Developed allergies.
Attended a number of fine schools.
Fought in one of the wars.
Designed the Winter Museum.
Avoided surprise. Dressed well.
Lacked political motivation.
Married once, loved much.
Threatened by habitat loss.
Chose wisely. Acquired taste.
Traveled often by rail.
Grew ill with tuberculosis.
We want what we want—
an easy path, a sunlit field.

The Wikipedia Page "Clowns Who Committed Suicide" Has Been Deleted

Community standards to uphold. Red rubber noses to thumb.
And so many questions about process. Do you remove

the humongous shoes before kicking away the chair? Wash away
white grease paint before placing muzzle to temple? Wig,

polka-dot bow tie, oversized glasses? How many versions
of a self fit into a tiny car before you connect hose to tailpipe?

I make light of my own pain because it's all I know how to do.
Blame my cartoon tears, the awkward orange light in this tent,

the decade I grew up in: all those packs of Marlboros
I bought for my mother while she idled

in a station wagon jammed with sniffling siblings. Or the pot
my father grew along the back fence, the babysitters in hot pants,

The Joy of Sex on the bedside table. We would have
bet the future looked like Pong, all pixilation and promise

and just enough danger to be interesting:
we rode across country standing up in the front seat

between squabbling parents, we were missiles
ready to be launched at slightest tap of brake or hint

of international incident. We knew staying safe
meant huddling on hallway carpet with hands on head

and holy shit, you should have seen that carpet—
ten years of brown and green and orange shag,

plus all the wall-hangings, we are a generation
intimate with macramé. You think I'm telling stories

now, that this would be better off as prose,
but let me tell you something real, and pay attention

because I don't do this often: every line breaks
somewhere. It's no wonder we grew up and gave

our children everything they asked for. It's no wonder
we want a pill for every ill and mistrust our institutions,

though we're either lying or mistaken because we believe
everything we've ever read or heard or seen or swallowed:

kick center-pole from under tent one hundred times,
we still take it on faith when they say it won't happen again.

It's no wonder we made a career out of this costume party:
say the word and we'll play the fool, provide the distraction

that enables someone else's sleight of hand, we'll carry
the ringmasters' top-hats. It's no surprise

our closing act falls short of significance.

The Letter X Chooses His Own Adventures

1.
You grow up along an endless sidewalk, the Midwest
playing on a loop, all cornfield and heavy metal

and the regurgitated taste of desire. The circle
and the circle back. Familiarity is the first step

toward trust—trust the only path to betrayal.
It's the neighborhood that makes you feel safe,

the basement where light bulbs burn out first.
If biology determines outcome, hide under the bed.

If you climb into the back of the van
the story ends here. Another begins.

2.
You learn what it means to crave
while snuggling in the back row of American history

or posing like lovers on the bumper of a muscle car.
You share hairspray and cigarettes, curls of smoke

and vodka kisses. You have nothing
and share all of it. You believe in Manifest Destiny—

her body is a continent. If you don't answer
just this one phone call, if you aren't around

tonight, if someone else drives her home,
if it rains, if it rains, if it rains.

3.
You move away but cannot move on. The landscape
never changes. North Florida is eastern Indiana

with a short-term memory problem.
The only kind of anger worth holding in your fist

breaks like thin ice. It's not supposed to snow
this far south. How long since you cooked

a meal worth eating? You can
spend the night anywhere. A stranger's

just someone who hasn't fucked you yet,
unless the truth is the other way around.

If you decide no one will get hurt,
write the check. If you decide to run, run fast.

If you have to blame someone
there are plenty of choices.

4.
Every war belongs to someone else,
camouflage can't hide what matters.

The sand is different. The waste
remains waste. The blood is the same color,

the sun just as forgiving. You will tell people
you are becoming a man. You will suggest

your priorities have ordered themselves
at last. It is the clatter and the power

and guns. No point in pretending otherwise.
If the other guy shoots first, get it on tape.

If you do not like the results, rewrite it.
If you do not like the smell, too bad.

If you survive, remember to remember
how bright this sky, how beautiful this moment.

5.

A guitar in your hands and someone listening—
why did it take you so long to arrive?

You hope it's the music but again the noise,
the drowning out. It feels

like waiting. That's the beauty of song:
impermanence. If you forget the lyrics,

swim. If you wake up feeling trapped,
swim. If your dreams begin making sense,

swim. If you cannot swim, wrap your arms
around any limb that passes amid the swirl.

6.
It's the repetition that kills you. It's the repetition
that keeps you alive. It's not the job

but losing it. It's not the sense of purpose
but the way grass creeps onto the sidewalk,

given time and water and sunlight.
Having money in your pocket

always felt like an undeserved surprise
so its absence doesn't hurt. What hurts

is having people depend on you,
this too an undeserved surprise.

If you let them down, turn the page.
If you let them down again, turn the page.

7.
There is always more than one possibility
but that doesn't mean happiness.

Your father dying, your daughter in trouble—
these are synonyms for helpless.

The human body is smaller and more fragile
than you ever knew. If you are allowed to vanish,

do so. If a migraine is born behind your eyes, seek
comfort in the familiar grip of a hammer handle.

8.
Make a world of your own choosing.
A place to eat, a place to rest—

all else is indulgence. You cannot believe
everyone doesn't gamble like this.

If you are out of timeouts, hurry to the line.
If you are surprised by how much weight

you've gained, grow a beard.
If you are afraid of flying, double down.

9.
Everyone dies. What's ridiculous
is it startles us every time.

Cheat on your wife, buy a motorcycle,
pay your taxes on time—we control

only what we control. You can try
to make sense of the sections,

look for order, impose rules,
you can sign the lyrical contract,

sometimes you will guess right. Sometimes
the leaves fall, and sometimes they fall into place.

If the sidewalk appears to end, turn left.
If the sky is wide, the story closes here.

If your favorite shape is a circle, keep reading,
but do not say you were not warned.

Work: an Elegy

Work for the rope it puts in your arms,
the flex, the strut, the satisfaction
of stopping. Work for the last slice of moon,
the single cold beer, work
because disappointing those who need you
is the only sin, because laziness
will not soon be forgiven.
Work for the month you spent
folded into the tail of a plane over North Africa,
for the scarves you mailed home.
Work for the taking apart,
the putting together,
the filling in. Work for the lantern,
the flame, the anticipation of flame
in the instant before a cigarette,
work for the woman waiting
in the kitchen you tiled
between the walls you lathed.
Work for the son who
resents you and the daughters who leave,
work because work is a privilege.
Work for the Tigers game on the radio.
Work for blood. Dust. Ashes.
For the flashlight, the coveralls,
the well-worn grips.
Work for your father's absent praise.
Work for the scar you see in the mirror,
for the complicated tattoo you never got,
for the music of your youth,
for the lightning and the oak.
Work for the American automobile
that will carry you home,

for your foot on the accelerator,
for the shift and speed.
Work for the heft of the hammer,
the shrill of the nail,
the splinter and creak,
for the barn that will not build itself.
Work for rip and drill,
for angle and crosscut and dovetail.
Work because men listen to you.
Work for that night you held a knife in anger
and would have used it.
Work for the dark birds that have flown
into your dreams lately. For the river
they cross, the wires where they rest,
the pattern they imply.
Work for the rock that breaks
and the bone that breaks
and the sky that breaks.

North of Dowagiac the Human Body Is
98 Percent Winter

And ninety-nine percent bottles of beer on the wall,
lukewarm domestic buzz, wood paneling, neon horses
trotting in endless circles. God forbid

someone opens the door, brings outside in:
blustery swirling reminder of the wife at home tucking
my kids to bed so she can touch herself

in front of *Dancing with the Stars,* couch springs eternally
creaking, homemade hand job the best we can do
when it gets dark so early: this particular point in history,

the least interesting of times. Two stools down
a woman I've known since high school offers a smile
that's half-hearted and even less promising: what passes

for flirting in this weather. Her husband's second-shifting
at the plant and they're both supposed to be glad
for the hours: these hours: any hours. Because it could be worse

though it's not always clear how. Can't even smoke
in here anymore, all I'm asking is a little heat,
spark and pull and breathe in the poison I choose.

Keno cards pile up in drifts, numbers freeze together: loser
begets, well, you know. Time and a half's long gone and
    my jokes
aren't so funny when the punchline's always the same—

the bartender's polite enough to laugh for a while,
wise enough to know I cannot tip
but only tip over. At least the fall from here isn't far.

Below a certain temperature, flesh begins to fail.

The Saboteur's Grandfather

If when the questioners come for you
you're watching *Baywatch* with the sound off,
not for the flesh
but for the sand,
the saltwater—

if they hold your lifetime against you,
your skills, your strong hands—   .

if your grandson inherited your knack with a wrench
but not your fear of loss—

if his anger is of his own making, his unmaking—

if you imagine he is a starling flown into an airport terminal:
by its nature a temporary place,
but offering to the bird
no escape once entered—

if you run out of words
for *disappearance,* for *blame*—

if they send you home to find
the front door swung open,
every bulb left blazing—

so much light, so very like a prayer.

Elegy with "Satisfaction" Playing in the Background

Life is assembled from the splinters and shards
of the broken things we never get around to replacing,

repairing, discarding. It's remarkable,
the flaws we learn to live with. This music

is not of your generation, or mine, and the Stones
never did replace that fuzzed-up guitar intro

with the horn section Keith Richards imagined.
Tempting to suggest art demands such re-visioning,

that meaning rises unbidden from initial impulses.
That the holes we dig in the back yard,

the creosote-coated poles we lower into them,
the woodshed or chicken coop

we never build around them—that these things
matters less than the calloused hand, the aching muscles,

a single hard-earned beer in the evenings.
That finishing the work is the goal but not the end

of anything. If you try sometimes
and all that. You are here to help me

because you've finished everything that matters
in your own life. You have been gone years

but I do what I can to call you back.
In your past are cigarettes and war stories,

a youth well spent when being young still meant
having something to look forward to. Back there

somewhere, too, the house you built
for your family: walkout basement,

above-ground pool, large backyard
edged by a meadow of dead grass

from which a single pheasant rises,
rises and disappears into the late-autumn sky.

4-F

You volunteer but there's a murmur in your heart, a stammer that might have saved your life. For a while, at least. You break another boy's arm in the state wrestling meet. You dream of the jungle. Classmates go, and their names appear on the gym wall. You practice magic tricks, slipping cards into other people's pockets and pretending to be surprised when they appear at critical moments. Everyone is losing faith; it's nice to keep some mystery in things. You start telling people that you faked the murmur, that you can control the ebb and pulse of your own body. It's remarkable how many doors remain unlocked, how easy it is to walk in and take what you want. This will not last, the flesh can hold only so many secrets. For years, the sounds will be all you remember—all that music like no one had ever heard before, and then the snapping of bone.

Six Years in Sudbury, Ontario

You will remember it as impossibly green. You will remember believing in self-sufficiency, physical contact, organic carrots, acoustic guitars, homemade peach wine, and whatever escapes memory you can invent. This was the point, writing your own story—plus, not ending up lungshot and bleeding to death in a jungle. Whatever doesn't kill you fucks you up in some other way. You will remember falling in love more than once, finding seasonal work at a camp store selling beer to vacationing Michiganders, growing your own weed, growing your hair past your shoulders, shrugging off all that disapproval—and so much water. Lakes around every bend, an easy place to drown or disappear, though nothing's ever so simple. What you will not remember is coming home, though it must have been something—crossing that spectacular bridge, five miles of suspended concrete and steel and the blood of the men who died building it because that's the way the world functions. All work is seasonal. Perhaps it rained that day. Perhaps you made the eleven-hour drive in nine and a half. Perhaps the driveway had been paved, the house repainted, perhaps all sorts of small miracles had happened without you. Was anyone awaiting your return? Did your father hug you? Let us say yes. Let us imagine that something went the way you hoped.

U.S.S. Bonefish

This is war: under water when the other side is in the trees. Support and protect, smoke break and missile launch. You will come home with four tattoos and still your father will not say he loves you.

36 Months in Waseca

Three years of noise, all bangclatter and howl. Three years to realize you've spent a lifetime dreading the wrong things. The worst imaginable takes turns with nothing you can't handle, same as all the other months. Tell everyone who listens you trusted the wrong person. This is the only possible mistake.

The Letter X Seduces the Asparagus Queen in Empire, Michigan

Do you know what would taste good with that asparagus?
Come on, baby, let me touch your crown. Let's
        overcompensate
for my split ends, your untender ambitions. Let's steam
and sizzle and deep fry, let's swim in powdered sugar
and funnel our cakes together. There's no shape we can't
        shift,
no season too short for arts and crafts and friendly
        competition.
You be my time zone, I'll be your western edge, we'll stay
light all night and tell stories about our dazzling
        childhoods,
angle of sun against big lake, a million smaller lakes and
        lesser stars,
the dunes and don'ts of having hippy-dippy parents—
marijuana growing under the elms and metalwork in the
        shed,
all that welding: joining of unlike shapes
in the name of beauty, or its opposite. Stem my tide, stalk
        me
all the way home, ride this highway until we hit the water,
the thing about a peninsula is there's only one way to run.
This is our saving grace, our fresh water, our reason
for eating. Sand on your tongue is part of the experience,
that grit and godawfulness, quest for absolution,
if you weren't young here you have no idea
what winter is—how quickly the human heart freezes,
how hard the ice. Once you've used a chainsaw
there's no going back. Let's wait for the lighthouse
to glance our way, spin and cycle and our moment of clarity

when all this paranoia pays off, let's pretend our piss
    doesn't stink,
our fantasies don't sink beneath familiar chop and heave.
This crowd is watching us, we are the attraction,
everyone wondering what you see in someone like me.
They do not know the high cost of symmetry, the value
of balance in an imbalanced world, it's not the heat,
it's the economy—ask about my good side,
let's show off our skin, capitalize me, let's shock the tourists,
these people who think purple is for vegetables,
let's pepper and assault and coat ourselves in cornmeal,
you lift your sash and flash your big ideas,
I'll spin and sidle and offer my strong shoulders:
first Empire, then state, then all the world's a cage,
surf and ski and a bucket of homebrew pale ale. As good
a place to start as any, here. The woman who created Barbie
grew up across town, Dr. Rubik—the cube guy—
vacationed in a cabin on the bay next to the Ford estate,
we've birthed a half-dozen serial killers and a trio of
    test-tube babies,
the dentist who invented invisible braces, that one girl
from that gum commercial, you could look it up, but don't tell
    anyone
because I might have some of it wrong. All my angles
wrench askew, the eight-cylinder engine
is the new endangered species and the planet
has never been smaller. All the more reason to give in
when I beg, borrow, feel you up. Listen carefully: never
wake a sleeping bear, never snowmobile alone,
don't pick the mushrooms on the eastern side of the hills—
these are words to give away, the price of admitting
that I am the ex among the wise, and as soon as I saw your face

I swallowed all your secrets. I wrote them, lived them, lost
    them,
I dreamed you into being. There is no path that does not lead
to this particular sunset on the longest day of this year or
    any other:
your cheek touching mine, this sharing of the air between us.

American Dreams

We suffer no shortage of examples—
our fantasies lacerated by the desire
to be on TV, to be seen
exactly as we are, only thinner,
perhaps ever so slightly more handsome.

A boy waits for his jetpack to be delivered.
A fire starts in a basement, a flood
is less predictable. Someone
makes change for a twenty,
someone else is making love—

odds are. It gives us something to talk about.
Even the most obvious mysteries
are worth solving. Something to do while we wait
to be ravaged by that actress:

the one with perfect teeth.

Ginsberg in Kalamazoo

After doing a reading for the rich kids at the liberal arts college, Allen Ginsberg ends up at the house my father shares with his friend Bob and whoever else is around. There's music and weed and Ginsberg is telling everyone that the scarf he's wearing is the same one Dylan wore on the cover of *Blonde on Blonde,* this tweedy-flannel-houndstooth thing. Herb Scott is there, trying to get Ginsberg to agree to take a look at some new poems, but Ginsberg is looking for someone to seduce, some Midwestern farmer's kid still trying to figure out who he is, cornfed and hungry for something new. It's not working out, for the poet or for the hypothetical kid waiting to be entered by the language of disruption. "This is a hell of a city," Ginsberg says to my father. "You've got to get out of here." My father, watching the evening unfold in a variety of directions, is twenty-four and stick-skinny and already surprised by how his life is turning out. You always know when you're doing something for the first time, but you don't know until later whether it will be the last or only. Even then, you don't know for sure. A year later, in this same house, my mother's water breaks while she's hanging lights on the Christmas tree, and that's when I enter the story, though I like to pretend I was here all along.

Self-Portrait as a Game of Clue

My grandmother in the dining room with the deck of cards. My grandfather in the garage with the red rubber ball on a fishing line that lets you know when to stop driving. My father at the front door in the purple paisley bathrobe. My father at the front door with the beard. My mother coming down the stairs with the white shoes. My mother coming down the stairs with the flower in her hair. Everyone in the foyer with the awkward silence. I am the invisible body. I roll the dice. I move. I suspect, I accuse, I open the envelope to see how much I've gotten right.

Leaving Kalamazoo

I am three and there are chickens in the back of this pickup, a makeshift coop. There is rust, and my father plays guitar. I will remember the moment as green, but it is October— already I lie about the small things. We drive south, away from a city of sliced celery, all back yard, above-ground pool, basement. At a stop for gas I find a balloon, unused, this small treasure. It is white, dirty. I am too young to inflate it. I will tell this story for years. Notice how I make myself the hero. Notice how I appear vulnerable while the world sings its blues over my head and the gear shift barks at my knees. Late-day light bends against the highway, and eventually the road turns to dirt. I am not sad we are leaving. Bridges. Rivers. The arc between: a shape no one has named. We are never coming back. I have learned the most important lesson this place offers.

THE LAST MOMENTS
BEFORE DROWNING

The Letter X and the Magic Act

Cut your girlfriend in half, she holds it against you for weeks.
Every time you kiss, you taste disappointment
like stale tobacco, raspberry wine coolers,
tattoo ink—all that passes for possibility. Pick a card,

any card—the man with the ax is wild

maybe because you're eighteen in a dark corner
of a dark parking lot, telling scary stories

while the dashboard light drains the battery
in your Firebird because you read somewhere
fear shares brain electrons with the urge to get romantic.

To smash the wristwatch is the easy part—
unless you return it restored
you have done nothing worthwhile.
Technique matters but the show matters more,

no such thing as cheap applause.
Stopping time's just another sleight of hand flimflam,
it's easier to creep yourself out than you'd expect,

and the various lives that stretch ahead

are more complicated and less important
than this moment
when your skin is an electric fence,

when what you want will never be this obvious again,
when you've revealed your secrets,

made your best case—

in that darkness, there might be danger.
To touch each other while we can is the only response.

Nocturne with "Kickstart My Heart" Playing in the Background

When a rock star dies,
the moon goes hungry.
When a rock star is reborn,
jolted back to the stage
by gasoline and guitar strings
and the kiss of someone else's
girlfriend, the planets burn.
There's no word for a moment like this,
for being in such a hurry
to love each other
that time dries on our tongues.
Driving past the cancer center
thinking myself profound,
I say, "Everyone in there is dying
or visiting someone dying
or trying to save someone from dying."
You ask, "How
is that different from out here?"

The Letter X Drives from Tallahassee to Orlando to Break up with His Girlfriend Face to Face

Angle-less landscape and still
I can't see what's coming—

something about the curve
of the planet, emptiness of the air,

not the heat but the humiliation
ahead of me. Windows down,

almost nine p.m., feels like noon,
soup-warm, small breeze, I'm rehearsing

though I fear that it's a bad idea,
that *polished* is a synonym for *insincere,*

so many other cars on this road,
I assume all of them aimless,

we are silhouettes in passing,
nothing more to each other,

avoiding eye contact, and I am tempted
to stop at Café Risque,

whose billboards promise hot coffee
and the stripping away

of the everyday obstacles that keep
one person from another,

as if flesh ever solved anything,
as if a bad pun will get me laid—

soon there's a toll to be paid
and I'm listening to music

from high school: rhymes
without consequences, one guitar solo

after another, all crescendo and crash,
every line, why, almost believable.

A Shrinking Circle of Light or a Growing Circle of Darkness

The sky swells to fit the season—
image skews to fit screen.
Okay. Start here: an empty field,
last season's crop ploughed under.
Beer cans along the roadside,
close-ups and freeze frames—
the components of visual narrative
are the narrative. When Jack Palance
couldn't get on his horse gracefully
during the making of *Shane,*
they played his dismount backward
in the final cut. You can fix
almost anything in post.
Griffith's greatest discovery
was the way a variety of distances
creates a more meaningful
scene. Go back to that field.
How you see this place depends
on the last time you tasted hunger,
how long since you were touched,
your own experience with such
a countryside. Sometimes
the editing is supposed
to be invisible. Sometimes
we are honest about our fragments,
our fault lines. You'd think
it would be impossible
to get lost in this field, to disappear
amid the frozen clods of dirt,
but still, it happens. A boy
climbs over the barbwire

and walks toward the horizon,
alone and growing lonelier.
The air closes in behind him:
a slow iris to let us know our part
in this story has ended.

Mourning

Last name, title, expiration date,
what goes sour, what survives:

we sort and clarify. Nothing avoids scrutiny,
her lasting knack for making us feel

untouchable. We smother furniture
in plastic. We come in out of the snow

expecting tenderness. We stockpile
all manner of miracles: cardinals

in winter, sun-catchers on sliding glass.
We lose track of how long

since we curled still and new and listened
to her heart keeping time—

it was the only sound in the world
and then it was not.

The Letter X Imagines His Life as a One-Night Stand with an Aging Country & Western Singer

I remember it as Knoxville but might have been anywhere
we could hide in public, holding hands in bland hotel room,

braced for some great storm. Nothing to feel bad about.
We ran out of cigarettes, we painted our heat on the walls:

tiny constellations in every fissure, loophole, technicality,
we could not costume over our mutilated potential.

I remember your invisible breath and breasts and tongue,
our strut and posture, the approach and invitation:

your fingers in my mouth, the switching off of the lights
and then back on: the closest we'll come to salvation.

Self-Portrait as Double Red Flag

In the last moments before drowning, the body
grows very still. You might look

at the shape of this silence in the water and think: *happiness.*

Think: *heron* or *peace.* You might remember your own failings:

those times you forgot the lift tickets
or could not pry straw from tree.

Isn't there a language that has thirty-eight words for *swim?*
This is the cue you've been waiting for—

you might think of one body against another,
each jostle against the skin, each electric shock—

imagine the spasm back to life, the throb of recognition.

How the Family Mourns Our Dead

We gladly share our Michigan, our Coldwater, our attempt
    at spring,
but hold fast to our grievances, our unspoken whatevers—
the weather won't change until someone fetches the pinochle
    cards.

This state is big enough, the town is small, the lakes deep.
Each of us privately thinks of the others as more loyal.
Each of us thinks we are the only ones hiding tattoos

under sensible clothing: barbed wire, roses, a drop of blood,
ink in the shape of a scar we never discuss. Family
is a history book full of question marks,

a scrapbook with names and dates redacted.
Someone calls attention to the cardinals at the feeder:
an excuse to talk about how beauty does not need us
    though shame does.

It is almost time to eat. At such gatherings, it is always almost
    time to eat.

It Occurred to Me Today That I Will Probably Die in Michigan

Maybe on a dune overlooking a lake.
Maybe during a snowstorm in a pothole
between innings of a Tigers game
on the front lawn of a Dutch Reform church
during the Cherry Festival, surrounded
by tulips. In this state we are never
more than six miles from freshwater.
In this state we are not fit to judge
the motives of our neighbors
but we speak with great authority
on the nature of pleasantness,
well-made furniture, skinned animals.
There's blood under the pine straw
of our history, bullet holes
in the city limits signs,
we created more perfect unions
then we laid everyone off.
My life here is my life here.
My parents met an hour from where
I sleep with my wife or stay up too late
to watch *Criminal Minds,* the same choice
every night, or at least the same illusion
of the same choice. Narrative
is a kind of cage as state lines
are convenient truth, plot hole,
invasive species. It's snowing again
and we're all complaining. Every hour
starts with a victim, ends with a rescue,
the opposite of all our lives.

The Letter X Puts on a Clown Suit, Sits on a Park Bench Across from a Playground, and Contemplates Fatherhood

Who knew there'd be all these questions? It's not the screaming
but the facial expressions that get you,
seven hundred ways to indicate disgust.

It's not the shit in the diapers but the changing that's difficult.

It's the smell of 3-in-1 oil that dials up childhood—
a black rotary phone on the wall of a garage,
that ring a surprise every time
and hanging up doesn't always disconnect your call.
It's the violently smooth handle of a hammer
and so many different saw blades:
teeth for every need.

You cannot make a thing without putting yourself at risk.
It's not the sweat or tears or even the blood,
it's how authentically you spit *motherfucker*
when your thumbnail rips off.

Build a treehouse to prove what?
That you know how to cut out a trapdoor
or where the rope belongs?
There's no such thing as a gift

but at least slides are no longer made of jag and rust.

Some things can be taught, or at least learned:
why a triangle's the strongest shape,
when to cut against the grain,
how to pluck chalked string against new wood

without leaving a double red line,
misleading and expensive. That's the thing.
Even wearing a rainbow wig, you pay for every mistake.

Possible Titles for a Self-Portrait at 42

Still Life, With Yard Work

The Rake's Progress From the Corner of the House
Where It Was Left in Late Autumn to the Back Steps
to Finally the Garage in Early March

Sorry Night (Or, An Evening with the Most Goddamn
Fractious Board Game Ever Invented)

The Boy With the Faint Impression Still Visible in His
Left Earlobe Because It Seemed Like a Good Idea In
1991

Portrait of the Artist Shaving His Beard Because the
Whole Fucking Thing Is Gray All of a Sudden

Three Musicians You've Never Heard of That Your Kids
Seem to Know All About

The Something or Other of Memory

The Letter X Gives the Inspector from the National Register of Historic Places a Tour of His Childhood Home

The kitchen is hard for me to talk about. The front hall
    speaks for itself.
Anyone would feel this way, growing up with eyelashes
    like a princess,
spiraling half into love every time I walked past a mirror
or wrote my name in the snow. No such thing
as too many ex-lovers or too few escape routes,
it's the porch light left on until the bulb burns out.
Yes, we have let certain things go. It's the only way
any of us makes it through the day.
Yes, these curtains are knit from cat fur,
second-hand choking: my grandmother died
between the couch and the hamster cage,
and yes, all this woodwork is original: untouched
planes of white oak, all dovetail and craftsmanship
plus four generations of initials scratched
with the pointy handle of a spoon. My mother
will outlive us all, she's in the Alzheimer's wing
because it's cheaper there and she likes the soup.
This carpet is her fault. The chandelier as well,
so much wrought iron and guilt.
I learned to scavenge early, spelling came easy
and I'd give anything to go back
and tell a certain version of myself how much easier life
might have been if I'd worn blue jeans more often,
brushed my hair. That basement door has been locked for
    decades,
some places just aren't worth the effort,
I've been meaning to go through these boxes,

sort the scraps, stay in better touch with my siblings.
The fire damage in my bedroom has faded. I heard
she married well. Maybe she remembers
how we laughed at this bedspread,
its tiny cartoon lassoes and spurs and horseshoes—
the way we tangled uncertain limbs and whispered,
as if being overheard was the worst that could happen.

Renaissance Man

Any of us may have something and not know it:
better someone else assemble the full picture.

 Each winter the same old man
 has a heart attack
 while shoveling snow.

Icicles form, stretch, fall. The translucent green plastic awning
  at the side door
fractures along the lines of the capital H

that announces our family name to the world.

 Years later. You are the old man.
 You drive south out of the snow.
 The heart attacks continue.

I am glad you're drinking less. I am glad
you have a dog, company
for those long nights on the road. I imagine
you must tell him about your marriages—

the long one, the short one, the annulled one.

The Man Who Lived with Wolves

learned that teeth tear best on dead flesh. Marking your territory means first drinking a lot of water. Play is meaningful. Candles freeze. The man who lived with wolves forgot about the woman he adored but could not hold. He forgot about attending her wedding on a Sunday morning in June and the smell of her hair on a sunny day. He thought instead about when to sleep. Where to eat. The man who lived with wolves learned his place in the world. Learned how to stay alive when the season turns cruel. The man grew to love the wolves; this did not take long, which should surprise no one. He wanted to stay in the tundra forever. He felt himself changing. Still, he celebrated with his last bottle of beer when the sea plane came to take him away. Back to a small apartment in the city crowded with memories and milk that had long gone sour in his absence. The man had learned, above all, that wolves do not need proof to accept possibility.

The Aging Country & Western Singer Imagines Her Life as a Series of Fruit Trees

Apple.
It's all about the eye shadow, shotguns,
dressed-up disappointments. It's all about questions
she never asked,
      or never answered,
now she can't remember which mattered more.
Summernight honeysuckle, lakeshore amphitheater,
someone important in the front row—sing

Peach.
as if her life depended on it,
though it's too easy to suggest it did.
Nothing more than flesh against flesh,
steam, the burning of leaves,
      the studio sessions—
wedding dresses, dark circles, cigarette voice,
eventually you forget which are symptoms,
which are signs of improvement. Whiskey
was never the problem. Not the only problem.

Pear.
There was that one man—where was he from?
Tennessee? Kentucky? Some state
like that, maybe with mountains,
or was it a town by a river—he was the one,
the one with the eyes, the hair, the hat,
thick knuckles and lips like hard candy,
but that doesn't
      narrow it down much.
It's essential to be able to look back
and point to particular opportunities,
roads followed, or not. It seems essential.

Persimmon.
Remove the stinger with your teeth,
suck out the poison. Salve the wound,
tease the scar, fight the wrong battles
so long as she never
          forgets the words.
She looks exactly like what she is,
and wouldn't the world be a simpler place
if everyone else did, too? There was blood.

    Cherry.
There was a green layer of scum coating everything,
there were headaches from all that enclosed air,
there were too many cities,
          too many songs,
too many hands reaching for her in the dark,
all those open mouths and no way to quench this thirst.

We Claim to Be the Only Species Aware of Our Own Mortality

We are predisposed to cringe at the sound of our own voice.
To shrink from unfamiliar touch. We do not walk into a room

intending to cause injury. We expect to leave witnesses,
we expect they will agree on the essential nature of our actions.

This is the unspoken premise of faith. We grow accustomed
to being seen but not heard. We rely on term limits

to provide frame, structure, ceiling, floor—unhindered,
      we drift.
We fear the undefined. The under-developed. We expect

that someday we will win the multistate lottery
or run into a serial killer as he's perfecting his craft—

we are willing to plea bargain away our principles,
we use words we do not mean. We understand our bodies

are drowning in hard seas: clots and cancers just waiting
for their curtain call. We are certain

someone has taken out a contract on our love affair:
a stranger will show up in our bedroom unannounced

as we lie spent and naked with windows open,
a comforting breeze. He will carry an open violin case

and specific instructions: one in the head, one in the heart.

The Water in Your Glass Might Be Older than the Sun

The New York Times, April 15, 2016

I'm pitching a comic book series about clown school
only I can't draw; I'm more the idea-generator. I've always
been good with the ideas. Can't you picture the panels,
all those blossoming young clowns in various states of wig,
grease paint, huge shoes? They'd always wear the red
    rubber noses,
even outside of class, that's part of the trope of the series,
that's how we know they're in clown school and not, say,
electrician school or meteorologist school
or the University of Phoenix. Think how much this school
would save on buses: use tiny cars instead, ba-dump-bump,
I could go on all day, but how have *you* been?
What's keeping you up at night these days? Did you
hear about how all water on the planet might have started
as part of a massive frozen cloud, drifting through space
until it hit our atmosphere and made our planet its home.
We're quenching our thirst with an interstellar gas
that's older than the solar system; older than this light
that warms us. I feel like everyone should know this,
that it changes everything, but I'm probably wrong.
No, let's go ahead and say it: I'm definitely wrong;
that reminds me, you know what's really creepy,
or at least, I mean, it's going to be once we finish,
is that damn clown school—can you imagine?
We'd need a trigger warning for the coulrophobic,
I'm not one to make light of anyone's fear. I do have
a question for you: should my clowns

also save the world? At least rescue kittens from trees
and whatnot. People like superheroes, or everyday heroes,
and would it really sustain our interest
if the stories were about merely the foibles
of clown-student life: the drinking and pairing off,
the breaking up and hooking up and homework,
and the red rubber noses, don't forget.

Update: 44

It's possible that—having reproduced—my body has
served its purpose. That all I have left
is keeping my nails trimmed,
hoping for sex,
etc.

Self-Portrait as Riker

It's not the beard. Not *just* the beard.
        It's that everything seems like such a big deal.
Like, propagation-of-the-species big.
        The binding of one person to another.
The need for genetic variation.
        The living up to, the falling short of,
the waiting my turn. The impatience.
        Love is measured sometimes
in depth, sometimes in breadth.
        The pleasure of cards stems
from that moment when I collect my hand
        knowing I am good enough to play
no matter what their faces reveal.
        The pleasure of cooking
is the sizzle of oil on a heated pan,
        the odor of unusual ingredients,
the anticipation of an unfamiliar taste.
        The pleasure of music is understanding
how each note builds on its predecessors.
        If my ambition feels inconsistent,
the fault lies in the writing—
        that fissure between idea and execution,
between language and flesh.
        Plans change. Vision evolves.
The narrative ever at war with the self.
        Every continuity problem
ends up visible. I fall in love often
        and never fall out. I cannot shake the sense
there's another version of me—
        taller, stronger, more handsome—
living some other life on some other planet.

Self-Portrait as an Aging Clown Going for an Evening Run on the Summer Solstice

Runner-up in a competition against myself—
blame these oversized shoes, this rubber nose
I've forgotten to remove. I've been losing
all my weight then regaining it. Better
than losing my mind, which is a one-way street
like this block where we've settled,
continue settling. What's
the word for _____? For _____?
Most of my unfinished romance novels
are about you. Well, some of them.
My calves are cramping. All the neighbors
are mowing. It's light so late,
we've had exactly enough rain,
we moved here for just such greening,
expecting meaning in how we shape
nature to fit between our sidewalks,
shape ourselves to fit somewhere,
anywhere. Someone has been writing you,
I've been sending the letters back
before you get home each day
marked NO SUCH ADDRESS. I've learned
to say yes only to things I'll later regret.
The moral of the story is not every story
has a moral. Or is it that not every moral
has a story. A season is almost over
the day it begins; yes, the implications
are unsettling, but what the hell,
can't stop now, too far from home,
going out always was easier than coming back.

The Problem with Burning Down
Your Own House

is shivering in the front yard in your underwear,
pretending you're as upset as everyone else
while the world watches; hoping no one smells
kerosene on your breath. The problem
with falling down a curving flight of stairs
is exactly what think it is: the soft spot
in your skull. There's a word for that:
fontanelle. This is not the same thing
as the smooth white coating on a wedding cake
though it's close. The problem with confusion
is the confusion. The problem with guns
is narrative inevitability: the ending, obvious;
the only mystery, how long it takes
to get there. Same problem with being born.
Same with falling in love. The problem
with passionate long-distance affairs is 9/11
and the subsequent need to show ID at the front desk.
I live in Michigan, which is fine,
except during winter, which is always.
The world continues to get in my way;
that is the problem with geography.
The problem with being white is you're allowed
to forget you're white. The problem with forgetting
is not knowing when it's happening.
The problem with cigarettes is disposal
of the butt; field-stripping's a lost art.
The problem with children is they do
what they're told, or they don't, either way
it's a problem. I poured a half-bottle of gin
into the sink this morning, the problem

with telling you this is now you want
to know why. The problem is, I can't tell you.
Motivation has never been my strong suit.
I also don't believe in intent; all that matters
is outcome. Not every consequence is intended,
there ought to be a rule. I was
going to say something about blood,
or bone, or flesh, but I am afraid
you would have gotten the wrong idea.
The problem is you think this is a narrative.
It's human, this need to find order where none exists.
Fire does not have this problem.

Rock, Paper, Scissors, Toast

Doesn't take long to get used to pointing at the palm
to indicate where we live now.

We like to brag about the produce.
We take credit for the lakes.

We are surprised when we realize
our children will think of this as home.

Lack of loyalty is the privilege of the new arrival.
This has less to do with any particular state,

more to do with the length of time it takes to write
    everything down.
Our grandparents die. Keep dying

until they are gone. At the funerals we blend in, say little,
compare shoes with the deceased,

play ridiculous games with precocious nieces, cousins
    somehow removed.
Toast always loses. Then why would anyone choose toast?
    Just in case.

The Letter X Imagines His Funeral

The glossy wood,
the smiling picture,

at the back of the room
a strange woman crying.

Earl Scruggs and Adrienne Rich Share a Cab to the Afterlife

Season's changing. Always. The only mistake
is expecting something more profound—
this vehicle could not be more ordinary:
dirty-yellow taxi, on-duty sign aglow,
driving just a little too fast through the confusion,
though not getting anywhere any sooner.
Previous passengers have scrawled names
on the seats and walls, making their marks
wherever they found room. Some with hearts
around their names, plus-signs connecting lovers,
flourishes under certain letters.
The driver has the radio on but we do not understand
the language. His phone keeps ringing
but he's considerate enough not to answer.
We deserve at least that much care.
Outside is cityscape, all heartbeat
and sidewalk. Outside is a mountaintop
thick with pine. Outside is noise
and weather and the skeleton
of our century. Behind us a cloud of dust
swells and rolls like the tide—
rooster tail, inflating balloon, invitation,
the ink and string and rhythm
of the ordinary, the beautiful, the both at once.
We have nothing in common,
only everything significant.
Our fathers are not waiting for us.
They are still somewhere in the shared past,
as we remember them, calling our names
and offering the advice they never gave
when we asked for it. Forgive us

for what we may have wasted. For anything
we did not get to in time. The road
narrows, turns. A hill is crested,
a sunlit field. The pattern grows restless.
The road is the illusion of a road.
Something has changed.
It's the season. We said that before.
A pen, quick. Let us add our names.
Let us say: we were here, once. We were here.

ACKNOWLEDGMENTS

I am grateful to the editors of the journals where some of these poems first appeared, sometimes in slightly different form or under different title:

2 Bridges Review: "Elegy with 'Satisfaction' Playing in the Background"
Arsenic Lobster: "Self-Portrait as Double Red Flag"
Booth: "The Problem with Burning Down Your Own House"
Camroc Press Review: "36 Months in Waseca"
Carolina Quarterly: "The Letter X Imagines His Funeral"
Cheap Pop: "4-F"
Cimarron Review: "Work: An Elegy"
Connotation Press: An Online Artifact: "Life Story" and "Mourning"
Crab Orchard Review: "North of Dowagiac the Human Body Is 98 Percent Winter"
Daphne Magazine: "Renaissance Man"
The Dialogist: "The Letter X Drives from Tallahassee to Orlando to Break up with His Girlfriend Face to Face"
FRiGG: "Six Years in Sudbury, Ontario"
Front Porch Journal: "The Saboteur's Grandfather"
Heron Tree: "Earl Scruggs and Adrienne Rich Share a Cab to the Afterlife"
inter|rupture: "How the Family Mourns Our Dead"
JARFLY: "Nocturne with 'Kickstart My Heart' Playing in the Background"
Lake Effect: "The Letter X Imagines His Life as a One-Night Stand With an Aging Country & Western Singer"
Los Angeles Review: "Leaving Kalamazoo"
The Mackinac: "Rock, Paper, Scissors, Toast"

McSweeney's Internet Tendency: "Possible Titles for a
  Self-Portrait at 42"
The Meadowland Review: "Grail Bird"
Midwestern Gothic: "The Letter X Chooses His Own
  Adventures," "The Letter X Seduces the Asparagus
  Queen in Empire, Michigan," and "The Letter X
  Gives the Inspector from the National Register of
  Historic Places a Tour of His Childhood Home"
Moon City Review: "The Letter X and the Magic Act"
Ninth Letter: "Ginsberg in Kalamazoo"
Passages North: "Self-Portrait as an Aging Clown Going for
  an Evening Run on the Summer Solstice"
Peninsula Poets: "It Occurred to Me Today That I will
  Probably Die in Michigan"
The Pinch: "Self-Portrait as a Game of Clue"
Pittsburgh Poetry Review: "A Shrinking Circle of Light or a
  Growing Circle of Darkness"
Poached Hare: "The Water in Your Glass Might Be Older
  Than the Sun"
REAL: Regarding Arts & Letters: "The Wikipedia Page
  'Clowns Who Committed Suicide' Has Been Deleted"
RHINO: "The Letter X Puts on a Clown Suit, Sits on a
  Park Bench Across from a Playground, and
  Contemplates Fatherhood"
Rockvale Review: "Self-Portrait as Riker"
Sixth Finch: "We Claim to Be the Only Species Aware of
  Our Own Mortality"
Storm Cellar: "American Dreams"
Weave: "The Aging Country & Western Singer Imagines
  Her Life as a Series of Fruit Trees"

"Leaving Kalamazoo" was reprinted in the anthology *Poetry
in Michigan, Michigan in Poetry* (New Issues, 2013). "The
Wikipedia Page 'Clowns Who Committed Suicide' Has Been

Deleted" was reprinted in *New Poetry from the Midwest* (New American Press, 2015). "It Occurred to Me Today That I Will Probably Die in Michigan" received Honorable Mention in the 2015 Great Lakes Poetry Prize; it was also reprinted in *Water Music: The Great Lakes State Poetry Anthology* (Poetry Society of Michigan, 2016). "The Problem with Burning Down Your Own House" was reprinted in the anthology *Booth X* (Booth, 2017).

This book was completed with the assistance of a fellowship from the National Endowment for the Arts.

ART WORKS.

National Endowment for the Arts
arts.gov

Thank you, thank you, thank you to my April pals, Todd Kaneko, Chris Haven, Amy McInnis, and Aaron Brossiet; and to the Poet's Choice gang: Dean Rader, Brian Clements, Christina Olson, Jean Prokott, Brian Komei Dempster, Judy Halebsky, and Ashley Cardona, all of whom push my work in ways I could not have predicted. Thank you to Ruth Foley for your thoughtful counsel. Thank you to my colleagues in the Grand Valley State University Writing Department for their generous and continuing support. Thank you to Gary Young for selecting this collection and to Michael Malan and everyone at *Cloudbank* for believing in the poems. Finally, always, and most of all, thank you to Ellen, Zoe-Kate, and Eli for making these words and this writing life possible. I am so grateful.